Secrets to Signing Up Your First Doctor

A complete guide to signing up clients for
a beginning medical billing service

By
Alice Scott
Michele Redmond

Copyright 2008
by Alice Scott and
Michele Redmond
Solutions Medical Billing Inc.
8251 New Floyd Rd
Rome, N Y 13440
(315)865-4299
(315)865-6359 fax
www.solutions-medical-billing.com

Other books available by Alice Scott and Michele Redmond – available at our website www.medicalbillinglive.com

"How to Start Your Own *Successful* Medical Billing Business" – written in 1999, revised in 2002 and again in 2007. For anyone interested in starting a medical billing business, this book is a **must!**

"12 Marketing Strategies to Grow Your Medical Billing Business" – written in 2002 and revised in 2007. If you've started your medical billing service and need to find more clients, you **need** this book.

"Take Your Medical Billing Business to the Next Level" – Are you ready to expand your medical billing business? Are you ready to take on more business or hire an employee?   Here are the secrets we've learned in the last 14 years from starting our own medical billing business to currently billing for over fifty providers.

"How to Complete a UB04 Form Completely and Correctly" – Detailed instructions on completing a UB04 form correctly so your claims will be paid on the first submission.

"How To Complete a CMS 1500 Completely and Correctly - Line By Line, Box By Box". – Detailed instructions on completing a CMS 1500 form correctly in easy to understand language.

"Mental Health Billing Made Easy" – How to make sure your claims are paid properly and you are reimbursed completely for your mental health services. Whether you are a social worker, a psychologist, a psychiatrist or a psychoanalyst, this book can teach you exactly how to bill out and get paid for your services

"Chiropractic Billing Made Easy" – How to make sure your claims are paid properly and you are reimbursed completely for your chiropractic services.

Table of Contents

How to Sign Up Your First Doctor

Introduction

Congratulations! You've made your decision to start your own medical billing business. Hopefully you've looked into it fully and are ready get going but what are the first steps and how do you actually get started?

Many people are tempted to go out and rent office space, purchase new computers, fax machines, software, desks and chairs. They think that they must have everything in place. But what should you actually do first to get this business started? What should your first steps be?

We all like to start with the fun and easy things. It's exciting – starting a new business. You want to tell people about it. You want to get your business cards printed up. You want to set up your office, order supplies. But wait. Let's get things in the right order.

You will need to have some things in place. You will need a practice management system. This will be one of your largest expenses in getting started. You must have a reliable practice management system capable of handling more than one doctor. It will cost several thousand dollars. It is a necessity. There are free softwares available such as Office Alley but if you are serious about this business you will need something you can rely on. The old saying "You get what you pay for" does have truth to it.

You don't need a fancy office. This is an expense you can do without until you sign up a few providers.

You will need some business cards. With the capabilities of computers and the papers available at office supply stores, you can make your own. Business cards are inexpensive so if you are not too worried about spending a little money you could order them.

You may want to make a brochure although that never seemed to accomplish a lot for us. Many offices would ask for a brochure, but it seemed to be more of a way of getting rid of us than something they actually wanted to look over. We much preferred to have the opportunity to tell them about ourselves in person. Of course, you don't always get that opportunity.

We now use our website instead of a brochure. When a provider asks if we can send them some more information about us, we refer them to our website. If they are truly interested, they will check it out.

You can't run a medical billing business without an up to date computer. A ten year old Macintosh won't work. Expect to replace your computer every 5 years or so.

You don't need a fancy office. This is an expense you can do without until you sign up a few providers. You can start a medical billing business from your home. You likely are starting your business without a lot of cash and need to start bringing in an income soon. You don't need a fancy desk and chair although that would be nice. You can work at your kitchen table if necessary.

What you do need is a client. Your first client. You don't have a business until you have a client. You must first market your business.

Most individuals who decide to start their own medical billing business start without much money. You want to start finding providers to work for right away to achieve a positive cash flow as soon as possible.

How do you go about starting your marketing? Find a method that you are comfortable with. Get your name out there. Approach any doctors you know personally. Ask them how they are doing there billing now. Don't expect that just because you have started a business they will be eager to give their billing to you. Providers do not change the way they do their billing easily. Even if they are not satisfied with the way it is presently going, it seems to be a very difficult decision to change the process.

Many people who enter this field come into it thinking that there are a ton of doctors out there who are just looking for someone to send their insurance claims electronically. Not so! Truth is there are tons of doctors who need an experienced biller to do their billing and outsourcing is the best option – BUT getting them to realize that is the challenge.

Many doctors are very reluctant to let the insurance billing go outside of their office. It really doesn't matter to them whether or not their bottom line is affected. For some reason they do not understand or care that you can bring in more money with the doctor providing no extra services.

I think for the most part it is a matter of trust or fear of change. This is their income. This is the way they have always done it. They may not be collecting all they could be, but they can't afford what they are collecting to be interrupted or mishandled. They must trust you that you will do a good job for them without a lot of "bumps in the road".

If they never met you before this meeting today it will take a lot to convince them that you are capable of handling their income efficiently. And we've all heard stories of bad billing services that leave the providers having nightmares. They want to make sure they don't get into one of those situations. But the truth is that with all the changes that have happened in the last few years, it is difficult for the providers' offices to be efficient at doing the billing in the office.

Once you get your first client signed up your goal is to do the best possible job you can for this doctor so he/she tells everyone about you. Ducks hang around with ducks. Doctors hang around with doctors. That's how you get more clients as your business grows - referrals from your happy clients.

One thing to remember as your business grows is that a doctor will not judge you on the problems that arise as much as he will consider how you handle those problems. You always want to be doing the best possible job you can for your providers.

Marketing was a difficult part of the business for Michele and me. I was raised in a family of eight children who were taught that children were "to be seen but not heard." Almost every stranger that walked into our house would say to my father "Gee Mr. Nemyier I can't believe you have eight children. They're all so quiet."

4

I grew up learning to keep my mouth shut and now I had to approach doctors who intimidated me and I had to ask them for their business. The other thing that I had to overcome was because of my inexperience with medical billing I wasn't even sure why a doctor would hire me to be responsible for his income. I didn't see what my benefits to him were yet.

As we grew, I saw more and understood our value. I saw that this was just too important a part of the doctor's business to not have someone in charge that understood billing and was good at collecting that money. And we got very good at collecting that money. I saw how the staff in the doctor's office was just too busy to spend 45 minutes on the phone with an insurance company to see why one claim was denied. I learned how to convey that to the doctor at the interview.

What I'm trying to say here is that if two shy, intimidated women start from nothing and build a successful medical billing business that bills for over 50 providers, you too, with help, can get to where you want to with your medical billing business.

Marketing Is Your **ONLY** Job

If you really want to have a successful medical billing business you must sign up that first client. That means you must put some serious effort into marketing. If you haven't had previous experience with marketing, start reading about it. You need to understand the marketing process.

Marketing is nothing more than getting your name out to the people who would be interested in your services in a favorable light. For example, people should be hearing about you as a result of the great job you are doing not because you got arrested for robbing a bank. You get the picture.

When you think about starting to market, you need to take these questions into consideration.

- Who are you trying to sell to?
- Where do you find them?
- How do you get to them?
- How do you convince them to use your service?

In order for marketing to be successful, you can't stop doing it. You always need to put forth some marketing effort. But especially now, at the beginning of your business you need to put forth a lot of effort in getting that first client. You are always looking for new ways to improve your business.

> Remember – You don't have a business until you have a client!

Some people tell me that they sent out 100 mailings and put brochures in some of the local shops. And now they are discouraged. When did they do that? Two weeks ago? A month ago? And they haven't heard anything yet? I'm not surprised. That doesn't cut it. What did you do today? What are you planning on doing tomorrow? What are you planning on doing next month?

Without constant marketing, your business will struggle. Marketing doesn't have to be a bad job. You can find some very fun ways to talk to potential clients. The important part is that you are very aware of your marketing strategies and keep your eyes open to opportunities.

Many people who want to start a medical billing business are working full time and cannot afford to quit their job to start their business. If this is your situation, you must find ways to market around your present job. You will need to find a few providers that you can take care of in your spare time until you are bringing in enough income to be able to quit your job.

If you have started your business and are working at it full time, you need to find clients. At least 80% of your daily work should be in the effort of marketing. Not all your marketing efforts will cost money, but some will. Make sure you allow a certain amount in your budget for marketing expenses.

You need to design your marketing plan allowing for flexibility as you find what works best for you. You must be accountable to that plan. Keep track of what your efforts were each day and what your progress was. It doesn't have to be fancy. You can write it on a calendar or in the computer or a notebook.

Marketing is a numbers game. If you approach enough doctors, you will eventually sign one up. But you must make the effort of the approach. Learn as you find new ways to approach the providers. Pay attention to what happens with each marketing attempt, at any social events and at each meeting.

Every time Michele and I met with a provider who was requesting information on our services we would meet afterwards and go over the whole meeting and our impressions of how it went. What we thought the provider thought of us. What we thought the account would be like for us. What we could have done differently. We tried to learn something from every meeting – the ones when we signed up the provider and the ones when we didn't. We tried to improve our techniques for the next meeting with a potential client.

When Michele and I started our business back in 1994, we were both shy and very intimidated by doctors. We found it very difficult to go up and try talking to a doctor especially when trying to sell ourselves. On top of that, we didn't have any clients yet so how good could we be? We had bought our second software package because we picked a bad choice on the first one. We had quite a bit of money invested and no customers to tell others how good we were.

Our first marketing efforts were chosen because of our fears. We sent out 100 letters. No one called. All right now what? I decided we had to call the offices now and ask if they got the letter. That was tough for us. A little easier than face to face, but over the phone was bad enough. We called 100 offices and two of the doctors were interested in more information. 98 of the calls were horrible for us but 2 were very exciting.

Would you make 100 calls to get two meetings? You would if you were hungry enough. Maybe it will be 25 calls for you or 125 before you get a "yes". It doesn't matter how many it is. You just have to keep going until you make it to that magic number that is the first one to sign up with you.

What did you do today?
What are you planning on doing tomorrow?
What are you planning on doing next month?

How Do You Fit It All In

If you are working at your medical billing business full time, fitting in the time for marketing shouldn't be a problem. As we mentioned before, at least 80% of your time should be devoted to finding a new client. Never mind shopping for office products or curtains. Find a client.

Marketing doesn't have to be a chore, it's a job. It's your most important job at this point in your career.

Let's say golf is a passion for you. That's good. Many doctors like to golf too. If you could find out when and where the doctors are likely to golf, you could golf at that course when they are likely to be there and maybe you could get to meet some doctors in the clubhouse. If you are going to golf anyway, you might as well use it as a marketing activity.

Or maybe you happen to live in a subdivision where some doctors live. Make friends with your neighbors. Check out any meetings that might be held in the neighborhood. Use any opportunity to meet anyone in the medical field. They may never use your service, but they may refer you to someone who will sign up with you.

Maybe one of your kids just happens to make friends with a local doctor's kid. There may be an opportunity to meet the parents. I'm just saying always keep your eyes open to opportunity.

You can't let your marketing efforts stop there. Remember 80% of your time should be spent marketing. There are many ways you can come up with to market and you need to be using more than one method at a time. If you need ideas for marketing, we suggest you read our "12 Marketing Strategies to Grow Your Medical Billing Business". You can use the methods we suggest that best fit your personality.

You need to always be improving and using your marketing skills. I'm sure we were shaking in our shoes at our first meetings with potential clients. We quickly learned that we had to relax. We also learned that we had to get over our shyness if we wanted to become successful in that business. We learned that we had to get comfortable with telling about our services and that we were capable of being good at it.

You will get better with your marketing techniques as time goes by. The important thing is just to keep working at finding those providers to talk to and learning to explain why your service will be invaluable to them.

One of the most important parts of the marketing process is being able to convey to the potential client how using your service is going to make things easier or better for the provider. Whether you are delivering this message face to face in a meeting or writing copy for a brochure you need to show the provider what it is that you will do that will make it worthwhile for him.

Until you understand yourself how your services are going to affect this doctor it is difficult for you to get it across to others. If you've ever worked in a medical office where there were bad billing practices in place, you may understand why a billing service could do a better job. But if you have not seen that, you may question why you could do a better job than the girls in the office could.

Understanding our value was a crucial turning point for Michele. She was into the technical aspect and at first she saw that technically the billing could be done in the office as easily as it could be outsourced. In some of our first interviews she couldn't see why the doctor would want to outsource. That didn't make us look very confident.

But after getting a few clients and actually doing some billing, it showed her exactly how involved and complex medical billing really is. Also, being exposed to some billing nightmares in offices and seeing how much money can be lost when the billing isn't done right helped us to understand just how important our service was.

When we realized that our service could increase a doctor's receivables usually by much more than our fee without the doctor seeing any additional patients, it boosted our confidence level immediately.

One office in particular really proved that to us. We had some inside information that this doctor's billing was in need of assistance so we pushed for a meeting with him. With the help of an inside employee we got him to agree to lunch. At lunch he admitted that he was not collecting as much as he should be.

It still took us quite a bit to get him to agree to let us into the office. A timely filing deadline was approaching for a large insurance carrier so we convinced him that he would lose thousands of dollars if he missed the deadline. We stated that we had the resources to get the claims filed in time.

He let us into his office on his office manager's day off. We accessed his practice management software and pulled up an aging report. His office manager had told him that the software didn't do such reports. According to the aging report he had a half million dollars out over 90 days. That was only insurance balances not any patient balances.

The report also showed that she wasn't billing any inpatient hospital charges and the doctor stopped at the hospital to see patients every morning before going to the office. When asked about this she said she didn't bill any inpatient hospital charges because "she didn't like the way the doctor gave them to her."

The report also showed she didn't bill any nursing home visits when the doctor's wife (also a doctor) visited several nursing homes and saw many patients. The wife wasn't very good about giving her the information so she didn't bill that either. (A beginning biller may wonder how you can tell that from a report. There were no CPT codes for hospital or nursing home visits.)

Another thing the report showed was that no Medicaid billing was being done. Medicaid patients were being seen but claims were never submitted. When asked about that, the office manager said that she couldn't get the practice management system to print out the right forms so she hadn't billed any Medicaid in years.

The last thing we noticed on the report was that no follow up whatsoever was done. Claims were submitted once and one time only. No claims were ever resubmitted, no electronic reports were ever checked. So basically they were losing at least 30% off the top.

Once we took over the billing we doubled his income in less than three months without the doctors seeing any more patients. Here is an example of what those numbers represent.

$250,000 a year in inpatient hospital
$125,000 a year in nursing home visits
$$35,000 a year in Medicaid
$250,000 a year increase by correcting ins info and f/u
$660,000 increase in income for year
$ 72,000 our fee
$588,000 extra the doctor earned just by using our service.

You might be thinking that this is an extreme example. Actually it is more the norm than you would believe. Many offices are losing that much money and don't do anything about it.

A lot of times the doctor is unaware of what he could be making and enough money is coming in to keep the bills paid so he doesn't have a clue. It takes too much effort to do something about it and they don't know what to do.

When you figure out how to show the doctor what he is losing and how easy you can fix it for him, you have a chance at signing up that doctor. When you see an example of such waste in an office you can then understand why you can do a better job.

You really need to get an understanding of what you will be doing and how it will help this doctor out when you are responsible for his billing. Then find the most effective way of delivering that information to him.

Marketing doesn't have to be a chore, it's a job.
It's your most important job at this point in your career.

Networking

Networking can be extremely helpful in signing up your first doctor. You need to find as many places to network as you can. Join any networking groups that may have people who are in the medical field. Join the chamber of commerce and go to the local meetings. Attend as many meetings of as many groups as you can. You never know when the opportunity may come up that will be beneficial to your business.

You may want to look into joining the Rotary Club or any Women's Clubs. Check out your local Better Business Bureau. Talk to as many people as possible about your business. You never know if the mother of your son's new friend is the wife of a doctor.

We once signed up one of our best accounts because we knew a lady who had her own marketing business and she told us that two doctors she saw were having problems. She told them about us and got us an appointment. We made sure we made it worth her while so she would keep her eyes open for other opportunities.

We've also signed up a social worker who was in the same women's networking group we joined. These networking groups are formed to help people like us find others interested in the same things we are interested in. People join these groups to find each other.

You may also meet someone in a networking group who knows someone in your field and will be willing to talk to them about using your service. My point is that you just don't know where your next lead will come from and you must get out and tell people about what you are doing.

Choices in Marketing

There are many different ways to market your business. How much of a budget have you allowed for marketing? If you don't have much to invest, you may want to consider a "hands on" approach where you are knocking on doors or making phone calls. Your budget may well determine the direction of your marketing.

If you have some money to spend, you can advertise or send mailings. You could get really creative and come up with a package to present to a potential office. But don't waste a lot of time or money on efforts that aren't working. If you try one method and it doesn't work, try another.

Some methods are easier than others for all of us and we need to find the ones that are the most effective for our needs. For us, being shy, it was easier to send out letters than make phone calls. But we soon learned that the phone calls were much more effective.

When we sent out our first 100 letters and got two providers interested we learned something from each of those two. The first one was an old chiropractor (soon to retire) who was having trouble getting his workers comp claims paid and he hired us for just his workers comp claims. We learned from him that providers are interested when they are having a big enough problem. We also learned how to submit workers comp claims. We didn't make a whole lot of money, but all knowledge comes at a price.

We were able to submit workers comp claims for this chiropractor and learn all the ins and outs of billing chiropractic workers compensation claims. We were so green when we started out that I'm embarrassed to tell you about one of the early mistakes we made.

When you file a workers comp claim to a workers compensation insurance company, you must also file a copy to the workers comp board. Our software did not have provisions for printing a C4 form so we were typing each form by hand on four part carbon forms.

We then put one copy in an envelope for the insurance company and one copy in an envelope for the comp board. It took 2 or 3 months to figure out that we could put more than one C4 claim into the envelope for the comp board. We were sending each claim in a separate envelope costing us extra postage and envelopes with each claim.

We were grateful for this small account which didn't earn us much money, but gave us valuable billing experience which we needed as we signed up bigger accounts. We got to make our embarrassing mistakes on smaller accounts that were probably more understanding than some of our accounts today would be.

The second response to our first marketing effort was a new doctor. He had just opened his practice and didn't know how he was going to get his insurance claims paid so he listened to what we had to say and decided to give us a try.

We learned from him that sometimes new doctors haven't figured out yet how they are going to do their billing and they are looking at options. This meant that new doctors were a better market to target.

This gave us some confidence and we started learning to try more aggressive forms of marketing – ones where you actually walk up and start talking to the doctor. I'm just kidding here but what I want you to understand is that if two shy women could overcome their weaknesses and 14 years later bill for over 60 providers you can too.

Some of the methods of trying to find new clients we've used are:

- Post card mailings
- Purchasing mailing lists
- Letters
- Cold calling
- Phone calling
- Hiring professionals
- Offering cash incentives to friends to speak to their doctors
- Networking
- Asking for referrals
- Advertising
- Answering ads
- Website
- Writing articles for ezines

- Article written about us in daily newspaper – You may be able to get an article written for you by submitting a well written press release. We were lucky. A young girl got an assignment to write an article about starting a medical billing business and called us.
- Worked specialties such as vision, physical therapy, and mental health
- Offering extra services
- Yellow pages

One of the things we've learned is that you never know where your next client will come from. It may be the new person sitting next to you in church or it may be someone calling you from a two year old brochure you left somewhere. You just have to make sure you put those seeds out there.

If you need more help in choosing marketing techniques, check out our "12 Marketing Strategies to Grow Your Medical Billing Business". We go into detail on all the different methods and give sample letters and phone scripts we've used. We tell you how to put each marketing technique to best use. You can purchase a digital download (e-book) or a soft cover copy at www.medicalbillinglive.com.

You shouldn't look at marketing as something that you do when you need a client. Marketing is something that you do every day if you want your business to succeed. It must become a habit that you exercise every chance you get to let people know what you do and that you are looking for clients.

If you are not comfortable with marketing, you need to learn to find effective ways that you are comfortable in marketing. There are a lot of doctors and other providers out there that could use your help. Marketing is just the way of finding those providers and convincing them that you are the person who can solve their problems. This is not always an easy task.

One of the things we've learned is that you never know where your next client will come from. It may be the new person sitting next to you in church or it may be someone calling you from a two year old brochure you left somewhere. You just have to make sure you put those seeds out there.

Develop New Marketing Methods

Don't rely solely on tried and true marketing techniques. You can come up with ideas for a new method that may work better than anything else you've ever tried. You can change a part of something that works for someone else and have it work much better for you.

Once early in our careers had a potential provider ask if we did credentialing. We weren't at that time, but we felt that if it was important enough for this doctor to ask then there must be a need for that too. We signed him up and Michele did his credentialing.

It was quite a little work on her end, but well worth the account. We had the time since we were still short on clients and it showed us exactly what is involved in credentialing. We now use credentialing as one of the techniques in our written marketing materials.

Also, if the doctor needs to get credentialed and also needs someone to do his billing isn't he going to use the person who does both?

There was another office that we knew needed outside billing help as we heard from many patients that the billing in the office was done very badly. We tried unsuccessfully many times to get in front of the doctor. We were friends with a girl whose roommate was a receptionist for this doctor so we told her about our need to talk to the doctor and offered a cash incentive if we could sign up the account.

She told us that Wednesday morning the doctor would be in the office early and we should come in about 8 AM. When we showed up that Wednesday she called the doctor out and introduced us. We got our chance to do our little sales pitch, but it didn't go too far. He told us that he was interested, but he would have to think about it.

We waited a few more months hearing nothing from this doctor. One day Michele had a great idea. She went into the office early on a Wednesday morning and asked to see the Dr. She used the timely filing deadline approach again. The deadline of this company was April 1 of the following year for all claims for the previous year. Michele knew that he was loosing thousands of dollars to this company because the claims had never reached the insurance carrier. She asked if she could run a report on his computer to show him how much money he was going to lose.

The report showed tens of thousands of dollars out to this insurance company alone. She told him that he had one week to file the claims to the insurance company with the April 1 deadline and that we could do that for him saving him tens of thousands of dollars. He hired us.

We scrambled!! We ran reports and brought them back to our office and started setting up his practice in our practice management software and entering patients and claims working day and night to get these claims in. We sent two packages overnight to the insurance company and collected a lot of money for him that would have been lost.

Keeping Track of How You Market

It is important to keep a record of your marketing efforts for many reasons.

First, it keeps you accountable. Are you really extending a realistic marketing effort? Are you meeting your goals? I hope you are setting goals. This is a must!! Plan out each weeks efforts and make sure you carry them out.

Second, you need to be able to see your progress. It always helps me to keep track of the results of any effort. If I made 100 calls this week and got two interested providers, I keep it on a chart. You can do this in either a notebook, on your computer, or make a wall chart.

When we finally got our first few clients, I made a wall chart and listed them on it. Waiting for new clients can be very discouraging so you need to do as many things as you can to keep your spirits up. Just having a list of the few clients we did manage to sign up would encourage me to go on.

Very few people who start a medical billing business on their own start out with clients. They must find them. As you've read over and over again, this is the hardest part. It can be a slow process and anything that you can do to see your progress is helpful.

Third, you may look back for a previous marketing attempt and the results. Many times we will get a call from someone who we sent marketing materials to in the past. It is difficult to remember all the circumstances that happened three years ago. Looking up what we learned in the past is sometimes helpful in meeting with the doctor now.

You may find in your notes that you previously learned that the doctor has had a girl filing his claims from the office on paper for 15 years and wasn't interested in your service. Now with some insurance carriers mandating electronic submissions and the new rules regarding NPI numbers, maybe the old way is not working any more.

You have a jump on it if you already have the background information. Not to mention that it might impress the doctor that you remembered speaking to him previously and knew what his situation is.

Fourth, to follow-up on possibilities. Once in a while you will hear from a provider that they are interested in outsourcing but are not yet ready. If you are keeping track of these providers, you can send something to them every six months or so or give them a quick call so when they are ready to change, you are the one they call.

If possible find a reason to call back other than simply "checking back." For example, it might be that his aunt who was doing the billing for 20 years retires so you call and ask if he has made arrangements for his billing after the aunt retires.

A provider may tell you that they will sign up with you when something in the future happens. It might be that a certain insurance carrier that they bill a lot of claims to starts accepting electronic submissions. You want to be able to keep track of these providers and sign them up when whatever it is they are waiting for happens.

If you know of something major going on in the medical billing field that you can make sure he is aware of, it shows that you are on top of things and you care whether or not he is ready.

On May 23 2008 Medicare began accepting claims with NPI numbers only, no more PTANs. Many providers didn't understand what this meant. Instead of calling to say "Hi this is Michele from Solutions Medical Billing. I spoke with you about six months ago and you said you were not yet ready to outsource your billing but you may be in the future. I was calling to see how it is going and to check back in with you."

Instead you could call and say "Hi it's Michele from Solutions Medical Billing. How are you? I was calling to make sure you knew about the May 23rd NPI only deadline coming up." Wait to see what the response is and then continue based on the response.

Now there is nothing wrong with the first approach and if you have no other reason to call, you should go ahead with it. But the second approach takes the doctor off the defense. You are not trying to sell yourself or convince him he needs you. You are just seeing if his office is ready for something that could disrupt his cash flow.

Anytime you can get a provider to have a conversation with you it is a good idea. You can show your professionalism and your knowledge and gain his confidence. If and when he is ready to outsource or switch services, you've already sold yourself.

Your First Meeting

How do you handle your first face to face meeting with a doctor? What do you take with you? What do you say? What is he going to ask you? How do you dress? What can you do to prepare?

First of all, try to be relaxed. You need to convey confidence. If you look or act nervous the doctor is going to pick up on it. Remember, doctors are people too. They sleep in a bed, get dressed, and eat food just like the rest of us. They are somebody's son, father, daughter, mother, etc. You get the picture. Don't get hung up on their title even if they do.

A lot of people, including us in the beginning, place doctors in a different class. Most doctors are actually very down to earth but some do get caught up in their title. In either case you should be professional and respectful but do not allow yourself to feel inferior.

I don't mean to keep dwelling on this but it is very important that you don't go into a meeting with a doctor lacking confidence and feeling inferior. Doctors are educated in medicine and you are educated in billing.

You need to know what you will be talking about and be able to explain it in terms this doctor will understand. You will need to be able to explain what your service actually offers, why it is cost effective for the doctor, and how and why you can do it better than it is currently being done.

Role playing can be very effective in getting you ready for this. Practice with a friend before your first meeting. This may seem silly to you, but it really improves your presentation.

You will want to dress appropriately in business clothes. It can be a huge mistake to look too casual. The provider wants to hire a professional. You also don't want to look like you are heading to a wedding.

The doctor you are meeting with will likely ask you several questions. It's a good idea to be prepared for these. You never know everything they will ask, but there are some standard questions you can expect.

How long have you been doing this?

Don't let this question throw you off. Respond with a statement of your experience with medical billing. You've worked in such and such office as the biller from 2004 to now. You left to start your own business.

You can guarantee this doctor that you will do an excellent job of collecting his money because this is so important to you. You've done this type of work for a long time and you are good at it. Use whatever your story is – please don't use the example I just gave.

Find a way to describe your experience and knowledge in the best light and offer all the positives you can think of. If you are just starting up, you don't want to say "I am just starting and I don't have any clients yet." You want to say "I've been doing medical billing for seven years (whatever your number is) and I decided to offer my services to other providers by going out on my own. Medical billing is a very complicated field and I am very good at it."

Can you send the claims electronically?

You really should be able to send the claims electronically because this is what most providers are looking for. They know they will be paid sooner and they know you find errors quicker so they can be fixed and resubmitted. Many providers choose to outsource solely to be able to submit claims electronically. You need electronic capabilities.

Do you bill for any other surgeons (chiropractors, psychiatrists)?

Have your best answer ready for this one. As you are looking to sign up your first doctor, the answer is going to be "no." You have to then add that you do however have experience in that field through whatever experience you can draw from. Michele would have answered "No, but I've worked for the insurance company for seven years reviewing and approving surgical claims. I was the one who decided if they got paid or not so I know how to get them paid.

If you are meeting with a podiatrist and you have no experience in podiatry billing, you could answer something like this. "No, I am not currently billing for any podiatrists, but I am very familiar with podiatry codes and I have been doing billing for X number of years." If you say this confidently, the provider will believe you.

How soon do you follow up on a claim?

Tell him about the system you have in place for tracking claims. Make sure you have developed that system and use it.
In our follow up system, we run aging reports every 4-6 weeks and we check on all claims over 30 days, unless it is an insurance carrier that takes longer than 30 days to process claims.

For example, Special Funds, a workers comp carrier takes 120 days to pay so there is no point in calling after 30 days. We answer this question by saying "We run follow up reports every 4 – 6 weeks and check on all claims over 30 days."

Can you clean up old billing?

Many times when a provider is looking to outsource or switch services it is because he has a lot of unpaid or denied claims. This can be an excellent way to get your foot in the door.

For example, if you find during your meeting that the doctor is still very hesitant, you can offer to work his unpaid or denied claims to show him how effective you can be. This can be the deciding factor in hiring you.

Other not as important questions you may get:

How many people do you have working for you? If it is just you, think of how you want to word this. You could say "Currently I am handling all the work, but I am prepared to hire someone when it is necessary."

How do you get the information from me? You should consider this prior to the meeting. Is the provider close enough for you to do physical pickups? If not, have alternative options available to offer such as mail, fax, email, etc.

What happens if a claim is not paid? You can answer "I check on all unpaid claims and handle all denials. If I need anything from your office to handle a denial I will ask for it.

Where does the payment go? Most of our providers receive the insurance payments directly, but we have a few that request the payments sent to us instead. Some billing services require all payments are sent directly to them and they take care of bank deposits. When you receive the payments, you are sure of getting all eobs where our experience is that some offices often miss sending everything.

What software do you use? State what software you use and express how much you like it or what it offers that you particularly like.

Can you give me any references? If you don't have any clients yet it is a good idea to have some professional references. An old boss or manager can write a nice reference as to yur work ethic and quality.

Do you do patient billing? Determine before the meeting if you will offer patient billing. We always allow the provider to decide if he needs us to do his patient billing or if his office can handle it.

How do you get paid? Explain your process to the provider. We always say that we run a report on the first of every month which shows everything we have done during that month on this account. It breaks down all charges, insurance payments, patient payments, write offs, etc. If we charge a percentage, we use these figures to determine the fee. We also tell the provider then that we expect payment in ten days.

You will usually get the opportunity to ask the provider some questions, too. You will want to be prepared for these. You may even have a list of your questions handy in your notebook. The answers you get to the questions you ask will be very beneficial in developing your "sales pitch."

Questions you will want to ask the provider:

Are your claims being submitted electronically?

How are you currently submitting your insurance claims?

Do you have a good tracking system in place?

What problems are you encountering?

Why are you now considering outsourcing?   (or changing services)

Do you have any idea of how much money you have out over 90 days?

The answers that you get to these questions will help you to determine how to sell your service to this provider. You need to figure out why he is considering changing the way he now does his billing, why he called you or agreed to the meeting.

Is he not bringing in enough money? Does he think he sould be bringing in more money for the patients he is seeing? Many doctors think that they need to see more patients when actually they just need to get paid for all the patients they already see.

If possible, try to get him to tell you what he thinks the reason is that his receivables are not high enough. Ask if his staff does regular follow up. Do they check electronic reports if filing electronically, resubmit claims that are not on file and take care of all denials?

He may not know, but by asking these questions you show him that you know what does need to be done. And if by chance, he does know, you know exactly what area to focus on when selling yourself.

For example, if he tells you that his staff does not have the time or resources to work aging reports you can tell him that the national average for claims not paid on the first submission is between 25% – 30%. So if his staff is not working aging reports he is probably losing 25% - 30% off the top.

Explain how you follow up on all claims over 30 days by running regular aging reports. Tell him that you act on all denials immediately. You check your electronic reports regularly and catch problems with patient's insurance much quicker that way. You want to impress upon him that you do not let claims slip through the cracks. By using your service he will increase his receivables by more than the cost of using your service.

Maybe the lady who has done his billing for 20 years is retiring? This doctor is looking for someone as reliable as his employee of 20 years. You need to let him know that times have changed. It is hard to find employees like that these days.

Besides technology has changed a lot and he needs to get compliant. It is great that he had someone like that for as long as he did, but now he needs to find a replacement and who is going to train the replacement? He is going to have to find someone who understands billing. How will he even know if she does?

He wants to make sure things don't change a lot – that his money keeps coming in regularly. You need to let him know that you are a professional biller and you will be able to keep his cash flow consistent and probably even increase it a little.

Has Medicare insisted that with the volume of claims he is submitting he can no longer submit them on paper? What is important to this doctor is that his claims need to be submitted electronically. You can emphasize that he does not need to take on the expense of updating his office.

Updating his computer system and software can be quite expensive. Besides you need to let him know there is a lot more to submitting claims electronically than a simple update. Is his software capable of electronic submission? What clearing house will he use? Does his staff know how to do electronic billing and do they understand all that is involved? Who will take care of the electronic reports? You need to get across to him that it makes more sense to outsource than to try to submit the billing in-house.

Does he have a high turnover rate of employees and just lost another biller? You want to let this doctor know that you will be around for a long time. He doesn't need to worry about you moving away or finding another job. He also doesn't have to worry about training you. You are a professional medical biller.

If he has a high turnover rate his accounts receivable has probably suffered. Now he won't have to worry about hiring another person to fill this position again. You can save him all the time of training a new person and he won't lose any money to an inexperienced person taking care of his money.

There are many reasons a provider may be looking into your service. You want to make sure that you are filling his needs. Focus on what his needs or concerns are.

If he is not taking in enough money make sure you are talking about how you will make sure his income will actually improve with your service. Don't waste both his and your time telling him how great your software is. Stick to what is important to him.

What to Take With You When You Sign Him/Her Up

What do you bring with you when you meet with a provider? You want to be prepared and make sure you have anything you might need with you.

Bring a notebook and a good pen. You will want to take notes of what the doctor has to say. He may ask for something you will need to look up for him or send him. He may give you information about how he is currently doing the billing. Jot down anything relevant and some of his concerns. He may not be prepared to make a decision on the first meeting and this information may come in handy later.

Your goal is to sign up the doctor for your services so you should take a contract in case it happens. You should have decided by now what you are going to use for a contract so have a copy with you. Our contract is very simple and is only one page. We actually fill out as much as possible before the appointment. If he doesn't sign, it is only one sheet of paper wasted.

Know your major insurance carriers in your area before you go on your first appointment so you are aware of their requirements. Medicare requires paperwork to submit claims electronically that you can have filled out in advance. Then the doctor just needs to sign it. Our local Blue Cross also requires paperwork be completed for electronic submission. It's a good idea to have that with you also. Being prepared says a lot to a doctor.

We also have a form we bring which lists the providers practice name, address, phone, fax, NPI#, tax ID# and any individual legacy numbers. If we sign the provider up we will need this information to submit the billing.

Make sure you have some business cards with you always!! If you have a brochure, bring it along. If you have a website, make sure the website address is printed on your business cards.

If there is anything specific to their specialty that you have, bring it. Perhaps you are meeting with a brand new physical therapist. He may be interested in the fee schedule Medicare allows for physical therapy.

Bring along your calendar in case you have to make another appointment to meet again in the future. If you have any reference letters make sure can provide them. The new prospect may ask for a list of referrals in his field in particular. If you don't have any, referrals from other fields are better than nothing.

Don't be ashamed or embarrassed if they ask for referrals from providers in their field and you don't have them. Don't lose your confidence. Just explain that you aren't currently billing for any but that it is not a problem. You are an experienced biller and you understand their specialty. The most important thing you can take with you on your appointment is your confidence.

Do a Great Job with a Smaller Provider

I've used the term provider often in this book because many people who file medical insurance claims are not doctors. There are many providers of medical service and equipment who were not required to get their doctorate.

Social workers, hearing centers, and durable medical equipment providers are a few of the examples of providers who are not doctors. We started out our business with single providers with small practices. They didn't bring us in a lot of money, but they gave us the experience of actually doing the work and bringing the money into the doctor's office. This helped build our confidence that we could actually do a great job at this business and they gave us invaluable experience.

Early in our business we signed up a couple social workers and found that to be a great field for us. It was very simple billing. There were just a couple of CPT codes and a handful of diagnoses. It was repeat patients so once we entered the demographics and the patients returned all we had to do was submit the dates of service. Social workers generally work alone with no help. Once their practices were up and running, they had a great need for help with the billing as this was not their area of expertise.

Social workers tend to love what they do which is counseling people and hate the process of having to collect the money they work for. Most do not know that there are businesses that are willing to do just that for them. It is usually a great relief to them to find someone willing to do their "dirty work".

Many of the friends of social workers are also in the mental health field. Ducks hang around with ducks – remember? When one social worker finds that she now can concentrate her energies on her work and not on collecting her money, she tells others, especially if she is happy with you.

We get many of our referrals from social workers. We once met a lady from NYC who billed for 21 social workers. That's how she earned her living. She didn't hire anyone else but these 21 clients kept her from joining the 9 to 5 crowd. Social workers are easy to find, (listed in the yellow pages) easy to sign up, and simple, uncomplicated billing for the most part.

They won't bring you in the big bucks that a surgeon will, but it's a great way to get your business started. You will gain confidence as you keep your first smaller clients happy and learn much about the business.

You will experience what we lovingly call "bumps in the road" and what's important when you do hit them is how you handle the situation. We preferred to learn these lessons with our beginning smaller accounts.

Make Sure You Do a GREAT Job

Hopefully you've worked out a plan for your business so that you have the systems in place so everything works like a well greased piece of machinery. Sometimes it is hard to get systems set up before you have actually got the work to do, but in order to do a good job you need to think these things through before the time arrives.

You will need systems for

- Getting the claim information from the provider – physically pick up, fax, mail, email, or download
- Entering the claims – Will you be doing all the data entry? Will you be able to enter them within 48 hours of receiving the claims?
- Submitting the claims – Which claims will go electronically and which will have to be printed
- Tracking the claims – Does your practice management system do aging reports? How often will you run them? How will you follow up once you run the reports?
- Storing the information - Do you have adequate filing space? How will you file eobs – by company, by date received?
- Sending secondary and tertiary claims – making copies of the primary and secondary eobs.
- Posting the payments – Make sure you understand your practice management system for posting payments.
- Patient billing – Will you send out patient bills monthly?
- Running aging reports – How will you check on the claims – phone calls, online, etc?
- Billing your clients – How and when do you bill them.

You can not afford to wait to figure all this out after you sign your first provider. You need to have at least thought all of this through prior to actually getting your first account. If you have a plan in place for how you are going to handle things you may still have some bumps in the road but it will be smoother than if you sign up your first account with no plans at all.

As you learn what is involved with each part of the medical billing process you can develop your systems. You want to make each part of the process as efficient at possible. Each time you incur a problem – or as we like to call them a challenge, you need to recognize that if you had a system in place for that challenge; it wouldn't be a challenge, so figure out a system.

Each time you institute a system you will save time, money, and become more organized. As you put systems into place you will see how much they benefit you and will enable you to do a great job for your providers.

Whether you do a good job or a bad job for your providers they will be talking to their friends about it. As referrals will be a huge part of the success of your business it is necessary that your providers are telling the other providers what a great job you are doing.

Some of the things you will need to do to make sure you are doing a GREAT JOB are:

- Make sure you check to see that the claims made it to the insurance companies. Read your electronic reports, set up a good follow-up system, make sure your return address is on all outgoing paper claims.

- Make sure your providers know what you need from them to do a great job for them. If they aren't giving you the required remittances after they receive them, it makes it difficult for you to keep track of the unpaid claims. If they don't include the ID# on the claims, you won't be able to submit them. Communication is very important with your providers.
- Make sure regular patient billing is performed.
- Keep accurate records of everything. Every time you call on an unpaid claim record a note in the patient's file to show what you were told and when. We enter our notes right on the claim screen in the practice management system.
- Back up your computer daily. You absolutely cannot afford to lose the valuable information in your computer so you must back it up regularly. Ideally this should be done where the back up is kept outside of the office.
- Follow up immediately on unpaid claims. Whenever you get a denial that doesn't sound right, check on it. Don't put it away for when you have more time. You never have more time. If you don't call on it now, when it comes in, you won't ever find time.
- File secondary claims when you are posting the payment for the primary claim. The absolute best time to file your secondary and tertiary claims is when the primary payment is being recorded
- Respond to any requests from your providers the same day if possible. If they request a report, run it then and fax it over. If they are inquiring about a payment, check on it then. Let them think that their request is the most important thing you are doing.

45

- Send your bills out to your providers regularly. If you do your billing to your providers on the first of the month, make sure they get printed and sent out. Some doctors are famous for not paying their bills on time. This is very difficult when you are first starting your business. You are probably depending on that income to pay your bills. It's difficult, but you must find a diplomatic way to make your providers aware that you must be paid on time. Too many of us find out way too late that some doctors have no intentions of paying. We have had to give up accounts and send them to collections – a "no win" for everyone.
- Go the extra mile. If one of your providers asks for something outside of the realm of your duties, do it for them as long as it isn't unreasonable.

Develop your systems as your business grows. As you find time consuming jobs, find better ways to do them quicker. When things fall through the cracks, find a way to plug the cracks. Don't be afraid to find new and better ways of doing things. And always be looking for ways you can improve the income of your providers.

Ask for Referrals

Once you get your first account running smoothly you can go to that provider and ask if he or she is happy with the job that you are doing. You can then explain that you want to expand your business now that everything is running smoothly with them and you were wondering if they could suggest any other providers who might be interested in your service.

Referrals from current accounts are priceless. These doctors are talking to each other about their experiences and you want them bragging about how good you are. Then don't be afraid to ask for that referral. Ask if it would be alright to mention their name when you approach the new provider. It is always better to have an "in" when calling on a provider for the first time.

Ask for referrals from anyone you can think of, not just the current accounts you have signed up. If you have a computer repairman who also works on computers at various doctor's offices, ask if he knows of anyone who could use your service. If your neighbor's son is now graduating from school as a physical therapist, ask if she will see if he would be interested in using your services.

I'm sure by now you get the idea. You need to let everyone know what you are doing and that you are looking for new clients. Even after you are in business for years, you will lose some of your accounts and need to find new ones. We've had doctors retire, doctors die, doctors get arrested, and doctors move away. Things are always changing. Remember that marketing is a never ending ongoing process.

Get Your Name in the Newspaper

Any free advertising you can get is great. One way to get some free advertising is to write a press release. If you don't know anything about press releases, it is easy to find free articles by googling "writing a press release". You can write one about your starting your new business.

We had a student reporter approach us once about writing an article about us starting our medical billing business. She did a great job and included a photo of all of us and it got us a lot of interest. If you are ever offered an opportunity like that make sure you take it.

Some Chamber of Commerce offices will give you your first $ of sales in a frame and the newspaper will put a photo of them giving you this honor in the paper. It might be worth the cost of joining the Chamber for the free advertising. Many times there are other members of the Chamber of Commerce who will be valuable assets to you as well.

You can also advertise your services in a display ad. You may want to target medical journals for an ad.

Signing Up More Clients

Once you've signed up your first client, you can move on to the second and third. They are much easier. You've gotten past that fear that you'll never sign a provider. As you add providers to your service, you will find that they come easier and easier. Once you've established that you are a great service the word will spread.

When you've signed up your first client, you now have someone to ask for a referral that can let others know that you are serious about your job and that you are good at it.

Once you've signed up your first client, you have sent some claims and gotten them paid and know that your system works. You have learned about your software. You have gained some confidence. You have gotten some experience.

You may want to try to find new clients in the same field as your first one. Surgery billing is much different than billing for a family practice. Billing for physical therapy is much different than billing for a pair of glasses. Having three providers in the same field will be less learning on your end than three providers in three different fields.

Of course as you grow, you will want to expand and probably take on more specialties. Each specialty comes with different codes, modifiers, rules, problems and new things to learn. But don't let that deter you from expanding. Once you understand billing, learning other fields is not that big of a deal. Different codes, different rules, same principles.

Work through each of these challenges as you come to them. The important thing is to know where to go for information when you need it. Don't get too worried about taking on a podiatrist when you've never billed for one before. You'll learn as you go along. There are medical billing forums you can go to when you have a technical question. We monitor ours daily and others have been a great help in answering questions. You can find our medical billing forum at
http://www.medicalbillinglive.com/members/

Each time we took on a new specialty I worried at first about what we didn't know and would need to learn, but I've always been surprised at the ease that we learned what we needed to know. When there is a will there is a way.

Wrapping It Up

By far, getting clients is the most challenging part of starting a medical billing business. It took us many interviews over several years to figure out what the secrets were of signing up providers.

When we first started we were lucky if we signed up one provider out of 10 meetings. Now when we go into a meeting, we go in expecting to sign the provider at the meeting. Now, nine out of ten times that is the case.

We aren't signing up that many just because we have other clients. We are signing that many because of all the secrets we've revealed to you in this guide. We go into meetings understanding that doctors are people too, just like us. They have problems to overcome and we have solutions. They are good at being doctors and we are good at medical billing.

We also go in with the confidence that we could do a better job for them than they can do from their office. We know that now because we've seen enough offices to know what happens in most offices when the billing is done in-house. We offer a valuable service at a reasonable price and the provider will benefit from using us. Not all providers are going to sign up. Don't get discouraged by the "nos." Just remember this business takes perseverance.

"Winners never quit! Quitters never win!"
Best of luck to you in your marketing endeavors.
Alice & Michele

39743417R00035

Made in the USA
Middletown, DE
24 January 2017